D0600689

56

NO LONGER PROPERTY OF
GLENDALE LIBRARY,
ARTS & CULTURE DEPT.

HOW THE CONSTITUTION WAS CREATED

THE U.S. GOVERNMENT
HOW IT WORKS

★ ★ ★

j
342.7302
HUB

THE U.S. GOVERNMENT
HOW IT WORKS

HOW THE CONSTITUTION WAS CREATED

JANET HUBBARD-BROWN

CHELSEA HOUSE
PUBLISHERS
An imprint of Infobase Publishing

How the Constitution Was Created

Copyright © 2007 by Infobase Publishing

All rights reserved. No part of this book may be reproduced or utilized in any
form or by any means, electronic or mechanical, including photocopying,
recording, or by any information storage or retrieval system, without
permission in writing from the publisher. For information, contact:

Chelsea House
An imprint of Infobase Publishing
132 West 31st Street
New York, NY 10001

Library of Congress Cataloging-in-Publication Data

Hubbard-Brown, Janet.
  How the constitution was created / Janet Hubbard-Brown.
      p. cm. — (The U.S. government: how it works)
  Includes bibliographical references and index.
  ISBN-13: 978-0-7910-9420-4 (hardcover)
  ISBN-10: 0-7910-9420-0 (hardcover)
  1. Constitutional history—United States—Juvenile literature.   2. United States—
Politics and government—1783-1809—Juvenile literature.   I. Title.   II. Series.

  KF4541.Z9H82 2007
  342.7302'9—dc22   2006101722

Chelsea House books are available at special discounts when purchased in bulk
quantities for businesses, associations, institutions, or sales promotions. Please call
our Special Sales Department in New York at (212) 967-8800 or (800) 322-8755.

You can find Chelsea House on the World Wide Web at
http://www.chelseahouse.com

Text design by James Scotto-Lavino
Cover design by Ben Peterson

Printed in the United States of America
Bang NMSG 10 9 8 7 6 5 4 3 2 1

This book is printed on acid-free paper.

All links and Web addresses were checked and verified to be correct at the time of
publication. Because of the dynamic nature of the Web, some addresses and links may
have changed since publication and may no longer be valid.

CONTENTS

1

How the U.S. Constitution Was Created

It was warm and raining when the Constitutional Convention opened in Philadelphia on May 25, 1787—an omen of the hot and muggy summer that lay ahead. Delegates to the convention arrived by horseback and in stagecoaches. They had chosen to meet in Philadelphia because of its central location. It was also the largest city in America at the time, with a population of 40,000.

The First Continental Congress, in 1774, had also been held in Philadelphia. Outstanding politicians whose names are all familiar today—John Adams, Benjamin Franklin,

Alexander Hamilton, Thomas Jefferson, Patrick Henry, James Madison, and George Washington—met to restore rights and liberties that Great Britain had taken away. When Britain refused to meet the demands from that congress, the colonists called the Second Continental Congress in 1775. During this period, Jefferson wrote the Declaration of Independence and a group of colonists created the Articles of Confederation, America's first constitution. They also named George Washington the commander of the new Continental Army.

Now, with the opening of the 1787 convention, Washington, the six foot two Revolutionary War hero, was back to help his country—only this time in the role of statesman rather than soldier. Delegates to the Constitutional Convention hailed from Connecticut, Delaware, Georgia, Maryland, Massachusetts, New Hampshire, New Jersey, New York, North Carolina, Pennsylvania, South Carolina, Vermont, and Virginia. Rhode Island had refused to send anyone because its state leaders were opposed to the creation of a strong national government.

The delegates' mission was to rewrite the Articles of Confederation, the laws governing the country at that time, which were proving to be ineffective. One of the main problems with the Articles was that they gave too much power to the states. There was a national Congress but no chief executive or judiciary. It seemed to many people that the states had become separate countries; each had its own constitution, its own militia, and its own government. The states had even begun to create their own paper money, which differed in value from one state to another and made trade very difficult.

A total of 74 delegates had answered the call to the Constitutional Convention. Over the four months that it took to create a new constitution, however, only 55 delegates would make an appearance. On average, 30 delegates attended each day. They came from different backgrounds, but all were landowners and most were educated. They ranged in age from 26 to 81.

Thomas Jefferson was the American minister to France at the time of the convention, so he had to miss it. He called the meeting "an assembly of demigods." In his mind, the intelligence and leadership qualities of the group were awe inspiring. John Adams was serving as the first American minister to England and was also absent from the convention.

The delegates originally thought that they were gathering in order to revise and improve the Articles of Confederation. After some time spent on that project, however, it became clear to some that the Articles needed to be scrapped and a new plan of government created. As delegates realized that they had to create a new constitution, then have it ratified (or approved) by at least nine states, they became upset. Some leaders were staunchly opposed to a strong central government. They were afraid that it would take away the states' rights, for which they had fought during the American Revolution. One of the strongest opponents was Patrick Henry of Virginia, who refused to attend the convention. When he was asked why he did not support the remaking of the constitution, he said simply, "I smelt a rat."

The year before, James Madison had called a conference in Annapolis, Maryland, to address the issue of the national government's lack of power. States were not paying their fair share of the national budget, they ignored the authority of Congress, and they violated each other's rights, as well as international treaties. Basically, the national government only controlled foreign policy and concluded treaties. Very few delegates showed up in Annapolis.

Those who did appear wrote a report for Congress. In it, they stated that they thought another convention should be called to discuss the weaknesses in the current system. Congress and leaders in all the states would soon know just how weak the system was. A few months after the Annapolis meeting, economically depressed farmers in Massachusetts, led by 39-year-old Daniel Shays, rose up and demanded relief from debt. Shay's Rebellion spread to other states and included as many as 9,000 farmers. Congress was unable to raise a force to respond to this civil unrest, which finally had to be put down by the state militia. People were now frightened that an uprising like this could occur again. This event probably contributed to the much higher attendance at the 1787 Constitutional Convention.

A lot of responsibility rested on James Madison's shoulders, and he rose to the occasion. In later years, he was called "the Father of the Constitution." One question loomed large: How was a group of men (women were

In 1786, Virginia's state representative James Madison
(above) called for a conference in Annapolis, Maryland, to
discuss the state of the national government and the extent
of its power. With only 5 of the 13 states represented, the
delegates in attendance urged that another conference be
held later that year: a conference now known as the Constitutional Convention of 1786. For all of his contributions, James
Madison is referred to as the "Father of the Constitution."

excluded from politics) representing 12 different states ever going to agree on paper about how to govern a country filled with people who had come to treasure their individual freedom? A new constitution seemed even more unlikely when, once the changes had been written down, the delegates insisted on a unanimous vote. Everyone knew it had taken five years to ratify the Articles of Confederation, which had been drawn up during the last two years of the war, and even after they were approved, major issues remained unresolved. Now that the time had come to more solidly unify the country, the colonists were beginning to behave with jealousy and fear.

The first thing the delegates did was elect George Washington as president of the convention. He was an imposing man and greatly admired because of his role in the American Revolution, which had ended four years earlier. After the war, he shocked everyone when he did not use his reputation and power to his own advantage, but instead resigned his military commission and went back to his estate, Mount Vernon. He cut a grand figure both on horseback and in the convention's meeting room.

The room in which the delegates met was only 40 square feet (12.2 square meters), and it was stifling, especially for the Yankees, who wore wool clothing. The heat contributed to hot tempers. Some of the delegates started taking breaks and meeting in taverns and private quarters, which created a lot of informal dialogue. Finally, in mid-July, the heat wave broke. After months of meetings filled with debates that often turned into arguments, the Constitutional Convention came to a close on September 17. At age 26, Jonathan

On September 17, 1787, the Constitutional Convention initially adopted the U.S. Constitution. The painting above is one of many artistic representations of the historic event.

Dayton of New Jersey was the youngest to sign the new Constitution; Benjamin Franklin was the oldest at 81. When he leaned over to sign it, tears rolled down his cheeks.

The Constitution was written, but months of suspense lay ahead. Of 55 delegates, 39 had signed, but would the states ratify the document? Would conflict break out between the Federalists, who wanted a strong central government, and the Anti-Federalists, who did not?

The Federalists, who included George Washington and Alexander Hamilton, had to push the new constitution forward by convincing the people that this shift in power was important. Their foes, the Anti-Federalists, or Republicans, were more united than ever in their opposition to the document.

Should the delegates have the people of the country vote on the changes in the Constitution, or should they put it before the jealous state legislatures? Finally, it was decided that the delegates from the various states would vote, but in special conventions. It was assumed that the smaller states would ratify right away, and the larger states would follow.

When the members of the old Congress (which had been formed under the Articles of Confederation) decided to meet in November 1787, only two months after the Constitutional Convention, only five showed up. It brought the truth home: There was no national government. This supported the argument of the Federalists, who began to spread the word that, unless the new constitution was signed to include all the citizens of America, they would lose what freedom they had gained. The first lines of the Constitution expressed in noble terms what they hoped to achieve:

> We the People of the United States, in Order to form a more perfect Union, establish Justice, insure domestic Tranquility, provide for the common defence, promote the general Welfare, and secure the Blessings of Liberty to ourselves and our Posterity, do ordain and establish this Constitution for the United States of America. . . .

Patrick Henry, on the other hand, warned his fellow Virginians after the convention was over that it would be a mistake to support the new constitution. He cried out to them, "If a wrong step be made, the republic

The U.S. Constitution is the official law of the nation. Created more than 200 years ago, it is one of the most influential documents in the world. Today, the original document is located in the National Archives in Washington, D.C.

may be lost forever." It struck fear into the hearts of the Anti-Federalists, the majority of whom were farmers and laborers. They argued that they had fought a war over their rights to individual freedom. If they agreed to ratify, would that hard-won freedom be lost? On the other hand, they worried, if they did not approve the new constitution, would that be the end of the United States of America? Would all the states become separate republics?

The story of the U.S. Constitution's creation would take on mythological proportions as future generations looked back and realized how a few men meeting in a hot room in Philadelphia sweated, debated, and compromised over how to develop a constitution that would insist on respect and protection for the average person. Even those who are critical of the U.S. Constitution agree that its creation is one of the most thrilling stories ever told.

2

A New Constitution to Serve All

By the time of the Revolutionary War, 13 colonies had been created in America, each with its own special character. Men hoping to find gold founded the first colony in Jamestown, Virginia, in 1607. In 1620, another group of men and women arrived much farther north, in what would become Massachusetts, with the goal of creating an ideal church. They arrived on a ship called the *Mayflower*. Over the next 150 years, Virginia and the Massachusetts Bay Colony were joined by other colonies, which would include Connecticut, Pennsylvania, Maryland, and Georgia. Eventually, these pioneers had combined the

ideals of self-government, religious freedom, economic opportunity, and land expansion into a philosophy. Above
all, they maintained a commitment to the freedom to
make choices.

The First Continental Congress convened in Philadelphia in September 1774, where delegates from all the
colonies except Georgia met for seven weeks. It served
as the national union in the earliest years of the United
States. Those who attended were a collection of Puritans,
Cavaliers, Quakers, and libertarian Scotch-Irish. Some of
the men who were there—George Washington, Benjamin
Franklin, John and Samuel Adams, Patrick Henry, and
John Jay, to name a few—were to grow in their roles as
leaders of the new world.

At the First Continental Congress' gathering, each colony had one vote; no one could speak more than twice
on the same point without permission; and the proceedings were kept secret. Their purpose was to define the
colonies' rights under British rule and decide on ways to
defend them. They wanted to restore rights and liberties
that had been taken away from them. There was a great
deal of disagreement, for they were all still operating under the British crown. They created the Declaration of
Rights, which clearly stated that they did not want the
British parliament to have authority over internal colonial
affairs. They wanted each colony to have the right to its
own defense. Still, only a few delegates harbored any notion of breaking away from England.

WHO WERE THE AMERICANS?

Each colony had an elite class, which governed a population that was rapidly growing with new settlers from Germany, Switzerland, Ireland, and Scotland. The term *elite* does not refer to those who inherited their power and wealth, however, even though many of them were quite wealthy. These elite were a natural aristocracy—some of them, such as Benjamin Franklin and Alexander Hamilton, rising from poverty. Many were the first in their families to have a liberal arts education. Most were young and filled with passion and a vision for the future.

According to James Burns, author of *The Vineyard of Liberty*, by 1750, descendants of the Puritans populated New England; Quakers were in the Delaware Valley; Anglican planters and children of former indentured servants dominated Virginia and the Carolinas; and Scotch-Irish laid claim to the frontier. The many religious groups active in 1775 included Congregationalists, Anglicans, Presbyterians, German churches, Dutch Reformed, Baptists, Roman Catholics, Methodists, and Jews.

Most of those making their way to the Appalachian back-country were Ulstermen and lowland Scots; about 70,000 followed the Germans to America between 1730 and 1763. In 1740, a famine in Ireland increased the number of Irish immigrants arriving in America to 12,000. During the Revolutionary War, the general population dropped from 2.6 million to 2.4 million, but by 1790, about 4 million people inhabited the country. Of those, 750,000

The 13 original colonies included New Hampshire, Massa-chusetts, Rhode Island, Connecticut, New York, New Jersey, Pennsylvania, Delaware, Maryland, Virginia, North Carolina, South Carolina, and Georgia. Established by the British, the 13 colonies fought for independence, and on July 4, 1776, they declared their freedom.

were black, and 700,000 of them were slaves or indentured servants who had to work many years before they gained their freedom. The notions of liberty, equality, and fraternity were unknown concepts among these groups of people scattered over a 1,000-mile (1,600-kilometer) radius. Most of the people lived on farms within 100 miles or so of the Atlantic. Anywhere from one to 3,000 people populated each of the various country towns. Philadephia, New York, Boston, and Charleston were the main cities. Beyond the Appalachians, one could find some frontier settlers, and beyond the Mississippi lay unexplored territory that had been claimed by the king of Spain. Spain possessed Florida, and swamplands dominated the area between Florida and Georgia. Western Pennsylvania and New York were filled with uninhabited wilderness.

The Second Continental Congress met in 1775 in Philadelphia. They sent the Olive Branch Petition to the British king as a final attempt at reconciliation, but they began to raise an army and asked France to be an ally. George Washington was appointed as commander in chief of the new Continental Army. On July 4, 1776, the Continental Congress adopted the Declaration of Independence, penned by Thomas Jefferson. In the months that followed, Congress drafted the Articles of Confederation, a plan of government for a new nation, which were approved in November 1777. Over the next five years, Congress directed the war and tried to administer the central government, but because of the war, it had to shift from city to city. The central government was, in fact, politically and financially dependent on

The Declaration of Independence, written by Thomas Jefferson, is the founding document of the United States of America. It officially asserts the independence of the 13 colonies from British rule, and famously grants each American the right to "life, liberty, and the pursuit of happiness."

the states. There were achievements, however, the most outstanding of which was the creation of the Northwest Ordinance, which opened up the West to settlement. In

1783, the British were finally defeated at Yorktown, and they gave up the American colonies. Benjamin Franklin and others drew up the Treaty of Paris, in which Great Britain officially recognized America's independence.

THE PHILADELPHIA CONVENTION

The mood was uncertain when the Philadelphia Convention opened in 1787. (It was referred to as the Constitutional Convention years later, but no one would have called it that then.) The war had ended four years earlier. The fiery rhetoric of the revolutionary years had died down a little. The delegates to this convention were concerned after learning of Shay's Rebellion, in which debt-ridden farmers had rebelled against the government of Massachusetts. Many saw the rebellion as an argument for a stronger national government for America. Some feared that unless they did something, the growing population would start to feel hemmed in, social conflicts would multiply, and states might turn on each other.

Still, it was a surprise when Governor Edmund Randolph of Virginia stood before the assembled delegates to suggest a new constitution. The mandate for the convention had been to revise the Articles of Confederation, not to replace them. The goal was to ensure the survival of the experiment that had been launched in 1776. The notion of starting over made some of the delegates unhappy. Two decisions were made at the start: The meeting would be held in secret, and a simple majority (more than half of the votes cast) would be sufficient to pass the laws.

James Madison presented the Virginia Plan, which he had written earlier for the Virginia Assembly. It introduced the concept of a bicameral legislature, in which the

JAMES MADISON: FATHER OF THE CONSTITUTION

★ ★ ★ ★ ★

A short, frail man from Virginia named James Madison greatly influenced the writing and ratification of the Constitution. In fact, historians would come to refer to him as the "Father of the Constitution."

Before the Philadelphia Constitutional Convention, Madison graduated from Princeton University and worked at various positions in the government of Virginia. In 1776, the Virginians created a declaration of rights that called for a careful separation of government powers. They were the first to call for a convention to evaluate the Articles of Confederation. Through the spring and summer of 1786, Madison remained at his beloved estate, Montpellier, where he immersed himself in a collection of books—some sent to him by his friend and mentor Thomas Jefferson—on governments in ancient republics. He wanted to learn what made them work and what did not work. He read about sixteenth-century Greece and fourteenth-century Switzerland and went on to the Germanic confederacies of the mid-1600s. He wrote a paper entitled "Notes on Ancient and Modern Confederacies," in which he listed the positive and negative features of those governments. He also read *On the Idea of a Perfect Commonwealth* by David Hume. Through his studies, he began to focus on how human nature affected government. Madison realized that humans act out of self-interest. He knew that different interests and factions could not be ignored, but instead they could be used in such a way as to support freedom and the government.

legislative branch would be composed of two houses. His idea was to have a strong central government consisting of three branches: legislative, executive, and judiciary.

Madison could see that in a large republic, it would be more difficult for people of similar passions to join together to impose their will on others. He thought at length about how people change as they go through life. As much as he liked the idea that all humans are created equal, he also understood that people are raised differently, acquire different amounts of wealth, and form different opinions. Therefore, they group together differently. If many factions were operating, an informal system of checks and balances would begin within those groups.

Madison became convinced that the Articles of Confederation needed to be replaced, not revised. He was further convinced that the state governments needed a strong central authority to counterbalance their natural self-interest. Finally, he felt that, in order to protect individual rights and promote the public good, an extended republic was necessary to rid them of the tyranny of the majority that was occurring in the states. He was concerned about the rights of minorities and worried that there was too much emphasis on state sovereignty (or rule), and not enough on upholding natural, or individual, rights. In a republic, the people are the ultimate power, and the people transfer that power to representatives by electing them to govern. In the confederation model used at the time, states appointed members of Congress. When James Madison went to the convention in Philadelphia in 1787, he was well armed with new knowledge that would reshape the American government.

There would be a separation of powers, so that no one branch could take control of the other. The additional idea of the legislature being made up of two houses, one elected by the people and the other appointed by the first from a group of nominees submitted by state legislatures was considered. Finally, the idea of a chief executive being elected by the national legislature was presented. It was passed into law within days.

The supporters of strong states' rights, led by William Paterson of New Jersey, introduced the New Jersey Plan in the middle of June. It suggested preserving the nature of the Articles of Confederation, but giving the national Congress powers to tax and regulate trade. Those who supported this plan were trying to prevent the smaller states from being overwhelmed by the larger ones. Each state, they said, would have one vote. Delaware, New York, and New Jersey voted for this plan.

New Yorker Alexander Hamilton wanted to base the new government on the British monarchy and Parliament; he was of the opinion that the masses could not be trusted to elect good leaders. He thought that perhaps a governor, to be elected by the electors for a lifetime, might be in order. The delegates, however, thought this was too close to the government they had fought so hard to free themselves from.

Arguments followed. A committee made up of one representative from each state, with Benjamin Franklin as chairman, met and reached an agreement called the Grand Compromise. The House of Representatives would be based on the number of people living in each state.

The committee agreed that there would be 1 representative for every 40,000 people in each state (later changed
to 30,000). The Senate would have the same number of
members (2) from each state. Slaves could not vote, but
every five slaves were counted as three people. (The issue
of women voting did not come up.)

The branches of government would provide a system
of checks and balances. That meant that limits were put
on each branch so that one could not overpower another.
Using the Virginia Plan as their model, the delegates
worked through each article. James Wilson of Pennsylvania spoke up against the idea of an appointed president.
Wasn't the point to prevent a tyrant from ruling over the
states? He came up with the idea of the Electoral College,
which was voted down at first but later accepted. It was
hard in those days for people to know about the candidates, because there was no efficient way to spread information across the entire territory occupied by the United
States. The Founders wanted voters to choose electors
from their states, who would learn about the candidates
and make the decision for them. Every state would get
one electoral vote for each of its senators and one vote
for each of its representatives. No state would have fewer
than three electoral votes. The executive, or president,
would have veto power over the legislature and would
appoint judges, they decided.

Delegates were divided evenly over commerce, the
slave trade, land speculation, debtor relief, and paper
money. The arguments around the many issues grew so
intense that Benjamin Franklin suggested appealing to

the "Father of Lights" to shed light on their understanding. From then on, each session opened with prayer.

The Constitution ended up being a compromise between the slaveholding interests of the South and the moneyed interests of the North. The Northern delegates wanted laws regulating interstate commerce and, further, wanted only a small majority to pass them, and the South wanted the slave trade to continue for 20 years or more before being outlawed. Many of the delegates hated bringing up the subject of slavery, some of them clinging to the notion that it would end on its own eventually.

From May through the middle of September, the delegates worked long hours to create a four-page, handwritten document. As the last members were signing, Benjamin Franklin remarked that earlier, he had looked at the president's chair, on which a sun was painted, and wondered whether it was a rising or setting sun. He said he now knew it was a rising sun.

The delegates had succeeded in creating a consolidated federal government with powers sufficient to force obedience to national laws while remaining true to the principles of 1776. But the real battle lay ahead; at least nine states would have to ratify the hard summer's work. Were the federal government's powers too broad or too limited? No one knew for sure.

At the end of the convention, three delegates—George Mason and Edmund Randolph of Virginia, and Elbridge Gerry of Massachusetts—refused to sign. They were deeply concerned about the lack of a mention of individual rights, and wanted to include a national Bill of Rights, that

George Washington was elected as president of the Constitutional Convention of 1787. The Rising Sun chair *(above)* served as George Washington's seat for nearly three months during the convention.

would enumerate such rights. Their proposal was rejected because the delegates wanted to uphold state constitutions (eight states already had their own bills of rights), and because it was believed that doing so would give too much power to the federal government.

It can be said that, by the end of the convention, the new constitution incorporated the Virginian Cavaliers' notion of hierarchical liberty, the Puritans' focus on covenant and community, the Quakers' emphasis on tolerance, and the belief in free will of the Scotch-Irish. The most important powers granted to Congress by the new Constitution were the power to tax everything but exports; the power to set duties on all imported goods; the power to prohibit states from interfering with free trade; the power to create and regulate federal courts; the power to admit new states; the power to regulate the parts of the United States that were not part of any state; the power and means to help states put down insurrection; and the power to coin money.

In the process, though, the delegates had split into two camps: the Federalists, who supported the Constitution wholeheartedly, and the Anti-Federalists, who were opposed to the new power given to the national government. As hard as the Founders worked to prevent a party system, in this area they had failed. Though a book could be written on numerous leaders of that era, there were four who held tremendous sway over the minds of Americans. They were so powerful that they became symbols of the new country and remain so to this day. They are discussed in the next chapter.

3

LEADERS WHO BECAME SYMBOLS OF THE CONSTITUTION

George Washington, Thomas Jefferson, Benjamin Franklin, and John Adams are the primary symbols of America's struggle for freedom and self-rule. Alexander Hamilton, who was Washington's personal secretary, and James Madison, who considered Thomas Jefferson his mentor, never acquired quite the same stature in the minds of historians. Hamilton, aggressive and flamboyant, was the opposite of Madison.

These men, together with many of the other Founders, however, held the country together throughout the early years, until certain habits and customs became a part of the national culture. It could be said that, with their collective personalities, including their weaknesses and strengths, they created a system of checks and balances among themselves that carried over into the Constitution for a large republic.

There was a great deal of personal interaction among the American Founders. In fact, many of them were linked both through their families and through their political roles. They were influenced by the same philosophers. The book that may have had the greatest influence on them was written by a Frenchman, baron de Montesquieu; titled *Spirit of Laws*, it first appeared in 1748. Montesquieu had in turn borrowed much of his philosophy from John Locke, of England.

Some of these Founders had attended college together, and as they entered the political arena, they had dinner together, sat together through countless meetings, and corresponded with one another on a regular basis. Politics was a face-to-face affair. These men were trained in the arts of debate, negotiation, and compromise. They knew that what they were doing had historical significance, and they did not take the responsibility lightly.

Thomas Jefferson and John Adams were serving their country in France and England during the 1787 convention, but they were informed of the proceedings through letters. Jefferson had grave doubts about the powers granted to the federal government, and he expressed these doubts to James Madison. Madison, on the other hand, was working with Alexander Hamilton to create an expanded national government that had sovereign powers over the states.

GEORGE WASHINGTON

Washington was born February 22, 1722, into a family of wealthy planters. His father died when he was 11 years old. As a teenager, young George was greatly influenced by a book called *Rules of Civility and Decent Behavior in Company and Conversation* (a sixteenth-century set of precepts compiled for young gentlemen by Jesuit instructors), which had been translated from French. He copied 110 maxims from that book. He did not go to college; by age 14, he was working as a surveyor. He inherited his brother's estate at the age of 20. He married Martha Custis, a widow with a son and a daughter, when he was 26. Washington fought in the French and Indian War until he was 30, then returned to the family estate at Mount Vernon.

When the Revolutionary War began, Washington was appointed as commander in chief of the colonial armies. Washington was neither a great intellectual like Jefferson or Franklin, nor was he a brilliant military leader like Julius Caesar of Ancient Rome or Oliver Cromwell of seventeenth-century England. Washington was formal and stiff and not particularly comfortable in conversation. Gordon S. Wood, in his book titled *Revolutionary Characters: What Made the Founders Different,* said that Washington's greatness lay in his character, especially the way he "conducted himself during times of temptation. It was his moral character that set him off from other men."

George Washington served as the commander in chief of the colonial armies during the Revolutionary War, and was elected as president of the 1787 Constitutional Convention. Just two years later, George Washington took the oath of office as the first president of the United States of America.

Washington's status as a hero was sealed when, in 1783, after the peace treaty with England was signed, he resigned as commander in chief of the American forces. The world was stunned that a man with so much power was willing to give it up and retire to his farm. Washington knew it was an extraordinary act that set him above the rest of his countrymen. He became more aloof, which only heightened his appeal. Like his colleagues, he was protective of his reputation, especially his honor. He agonized, for example, over the Virginia Assembly's offer of land shares for his services to the state and the cause of canal building, for it would have made him a fortune. He finally gave the land away to the college that became Washington and Lee.

Whether or not to attend the Constitutional Convention in 1787 also caused Washington a great deal of stress. What was the right thing to do? He decided to go when he heard rumors that the people thought he wanted the new federal government to fail so that he could arrange a military takeover. He was elected president of the convention. James Monroe was certain that it was Washington's influence that carried the government. After the convention, he would be elected the first president of the United States. He would handle it all with great dignity.

BENJAMIN FRANKLIN

At age 81, Benjamin Franklin was the oldest of the political leaders at the convention. Like Washington, he was careful of how he presented himself to the world. His wit and self-awareness, and his many voices and masks, made him a difficult man to know. He was a brilliant scientist and a superb businessman. He made enough money through land speculation, loans, and various businesses

One of the Founding Fathers of the United States of America,
Benjamin Franklin greatly contributed to the developing nation as a scientist, scholar, diplomat and more. At 81 years
old, Benjamin Franklin was the oldest delegate at the Constitutional Convention. Due to his age and status, Franklin
served as a mediator in many disputes, and was one of the
most influential delegates in attendance.

to retire at age 42. His goal was to become a gentleman, and he did. It was an easy step from that role to the role of politician, but he grew tired of that and began to focus on England.

In 1757, Franklin went to England as an agent of the Pennsylvania Assembly. The truth was, he was loyal to the king. He remained there through the early 1760s and went through a period of anti-Americanism. He opposed the Stamp Act, which shocked American patriots, although he eventually came to support it. Over the next four or five years, he was in the position of being too American for the English and too English for the Americans. Franklin had hoped for a royal appointment in England and was shocked when he was rejected. He downplayed the looming problems between Britain and the American colonies until it was almost too late. He was viciously attacked before the Privy Council in England and called a thief by the solicitor general, an act that infuriated him. Finally, in March 1775, he sailed back to America and joined the American Revolution with a vengeance because of his anger at the British king. Americans had become suspicious of him, so part of his public passion for the war might have been to convince people that he was not a British spy.

The American government sent him to Paris in 1776 as a diplomat, and he excelled at that role. He almost single-handedly brought Louis XVI into the Revolutionary War on behalf of the new republic. To the French, he was a genius and he embodied the part of America that was primitive, innocent, and free. He made them fall in love with America. The nobility lionized him, and his face appeared on boxes, rings, and prints. When he returned to America in 1785, no one knew what to make of him. He had spent most of the last 33 years living in England

THE AMERICAN ENLIGHTENMENT

It is important to understand that our country's Founders were aristocrats, but they were different from the English, who inherited land and great sums of money, whether they contributed to their country or not. Many of the Founders were wealthy, but their kind of aristocracy was based more on merit and talent. They did not hide their superiority, but neither did they look down on the common man. They were part of the Anglo-American Enlightenment, which placed a strong emphasis on politeness, the source of civility. In fact, the word *civilization* is derived from the word *civility*. Gordon Wood wrote in his book *Revolutionary Characters: What Made the Founders Different*, "To contemplate aesthetically an ordered universe and to know the best that was thought and said in the world—that was enlightenment."

In England, thinkers such as John Locke and Adam Smith believed that civilization could be achieved, but societies had to advance through four stages to get there. To them, America was at the beginning stage. Americans were doing their part to become members of a cultural world. The people involved in creating the new America were quite focused on what it meant to be a gentleman (or a lady). Politeness, grace, taste, learning, and character were all hallmarks. To become a politician, one had to be tolerant, honest, reasonable—in and France. People knew he was an international hero, but they could not quite figure out why. They still had him pegged as a patriot and scientist. He played a large role in the Constitutional Convention of 1787 as sage and mediator.

other words, a gentleman. The eighteenth century was the beginning of the liberal arts education, an absolute requirement for anyone wanting to be known as a gentleman. A gentleman also did not work with his hands and had to act in a disinterested way to promote public good. *Disinterested* to them meant "not influenced by profit." That was a little farfetched, even to them, for several of them had ties to international trade. As unique as they were, they were human, and wealth and status had great allure for them. It was considered a duty and a burden to remain in a leadership position.

The Founders read books by Scottish philosophers David Hume, Adam Smith, John Millar, and others, who matched the American Founders in brilliance and creativity. All were familiar with England's Magna Carta, the charter of political and civil liberties granted by King John in 1215. How one presented oneself to the world was an indication of character. These leaders wanted to be effective in showing the world that they were living up to the values and duties imposed upon them by their culture. They hid their personal feelings to allow their public image to be recorded. Martha Washington and Thomas Jefferson destroyed their letters to their spouses for this reason. Adams and Washington especially understood the theatrical world they lived in and became experts at creating the proper image.

JOHN ADAMS

John Adams of Massachusetts, a graduate of Harvard University, wrote a pamphlet in 1776 called *Thoughts on Government*. This document became quite influential in guiding the Framers of the Constitution, and Adams played a large role in drafting the Massachusetts constitution in 1780. At the First Continental Congress, during the early days of the drive for independence, he had been at the forefront. He and Jefferson became close friends. They parted ways for years over their differing beliefs, but later in life they began to correspond once again. They were an interesting twosome, Jefferson, the Virginia aristocrat who was tall and lean, and Adams, the short and stocky New Englander who never minced words. Adams was the first minister appointed to England, and he became vice president of the United States in 1789. He was outspoken and cantankerous, to the point that his colleagues did not know what to do with him. He had a long marriage to Abigail Adams, whom many thought to be as strong as her husband.

As a political scientist, John Adams believed that government was closely related to society and that no state would be secure unless the two were reconciled. By the time the Constitutional Convention met, the Declaration of Independence had been in effect for 12 years. During those years, Adams had lost his faith in people. He no longer believed that a society could be egalitarian (that humans are equal, especially with respect to social, political, and economic rights and privileges), and this conviction

Although he did not attend the Constitutional Convention of 1787, John Adams was extremely influential in framing the new nation's government. A Harvard-educated delegate from Massachusetts, John Adams was known as a politician and a great political philosopher. John Adams served as the first vice president of the United States and then as president.

would distance him from the others. He also thought that Americans, like all people, were lacking in virtue. Still, he hoped for politicians who could mold the character of the people. He soon gave up that hope, as well.

At first, in 1787, Adams was uninterested in the Federalists' idea of creating a new national government. Once it was created, however, he strongly supported it. In fact, the resulting government was quite similar to Adams's own, earlier proposals for balance in government.

THOMAS JEFFERSON

Standing six feet two inches tall, Thomas Jefferson had a freckled complexion, hazel eyes, and copper-colored hair. He was intelligent, reserved, progressive, and optimistic. Born to a self-made father and a mother from the Virginia aristocracy, Jefferson attended the College of William and Mary and loved it. He was a man of opposites. He loved shopping and having money, yet he viewed the poor farmer as the ideal. He hated the focus on money-making and capitalism, but he did much to bring it about. He was a sophisticated man of the world, yet he loved nothing more than his mountaintop retreat of Monticello. He craved knowledge and read as many books as he could get his hands on, which put him at the head of the American Enlightenment. This movement focused on spreading light (knowledge) and pushing away darkness (ignorance). The virtue that Jefferson aspired to came from the citizen's participation in society, not in government. He penned the Declaration of Independence, and it

Thomas Jefferson was the principal author of the Declaration of Independence, governor of Virginia, U.S. minister to France, secretary of state, vice president, and the president of the United States. He is one of the most influential American figures in history.

was in that document that the phrase "the United States of America" was used for the first time.

Anything that encouraged discussion and dialogue was considered a virtue. The idea was to create a world where people loved one another. Together with this came Jefferson's utter belief in a minimal government. He hated the modern idea of a state, although he did believe in nationhood. He assumed that a natural aristocracy would rule the country, and he believed in the capacity of the people to elect that aristocracy. He could not tolerate the Federalist monarchists.

Jefferson's father was a wealthy planter who had married a woman from one of the first families of Virginia. It has always been hard to reconcile Jefferson's belief in the people and his notions of freedom with his strong prejudice against blacks. He felt they were inferior. He hated the notion of a mixture of color, believing it would destroy the national genius. He could not imagine blacks and whites living together, even though he was surrounded by blacks and was related to some through his father-in-law's miscegenation (sexual relationship) with some of his slaves. Jefferson also had relations with one of his slaves, Sally Hemings, who was the half-sister of Jefferson's wife. It is commonly believed that he had at least one child with her.

4

RATIFICATION AND
A BILL OF RIGHTS

Although the Founders worked to prevent the creation of political parties in America, the issue of states' rights versus central government made parties inevitable. Washington, Hamilton, Adams, Madison, and John Jay of New York were strong Federalists who had the daunting task of convincing states to ratify the new constitution. Madison had converted to Federalism while working in the Virginia Assembly. He found the members of the state assembly to be short-sighted, fickle, and greedy. He thought they made their state assembly too mighty.

The Federalists were not just a strong elite. They received support from merchants and farmers who wanted to get richer in the growing American marketplace. Generally, they were younger and more devoted to union. They were

optimistic and shared a faith that a strong central government could protect rather than endanger republican liberties. Their careers would take off after the convention.

THE PRESS

Much had changed in the press by the time Benjamin Franklin
attended the 1787 Constitutional Convention. He could recall his
brother, a printer, being put in jail around 1720 because he offended
the Virginia Assembly. When he was released, the British government forbade him from printing his paper, so Benjamin stepped in
and put his name on it.

During the 1780s and 1790s, newspapers were still filled with
news from the Old World, but they had become bolder on the eve of
the Revolutionary War. By 1790, there were almost 100 newspapers
operating in the country. Most were weeklies, but there were 8 dailies.
They were pressed down one page at a time on a crude block of type
by workers, then printed on rough rag paper. In essence, they were
two- to four-page news sheets. It is interesting to note that the column
layout and the general news ads were similar to newspapers today.
These news sheets were also filled with opinions and letters. The
modern-day editorial also had its beginning at that time.

Newspapers were expensive to print, so editors were in the busi-
ness of making money. Their papers were not objective in the least.
Most were obviously identified as either Federalist or Republican, and
it was common for editors to be sponsored by politicians. Thomas
Jefferson, for example, sponsored the *National Gazette,* and Alexander Hamilton sponsored the *Gazette of the United States.* Today
many of those editors would be sued for libel, but at that time, they
felt protected by the new Bill of Rights. There was no law against

The Anti-Federalists, who later became known as the Democrat-Republicans, included Thomas Jefferson, Patrick Henry, and George Mason of Virginia; Thomas Paine

plagiarism, and editors freely lifted material from other newspapers and anywhere else they could find it.

In general, the Founders were enthusiastic about newspapers, but there were times when they went too far. When George Washington was in office, he sometimes became furious over what he read about himself. When John Adams wrote "A Constitution or Form of Government for the Commonwealth of Massachusetts" in 1779, he included freedom of the press in the document. The most famous journalistic works of the 1780s were the *Federalist Papers*, a series of essays written by James Madison, Hamilton, and John Jay.

In 1798, when John Adams was president, he supported the Alien and Sedition Acts. Created by the Federalists, who were in power in Congress at the time, one of the laws stipulated that editors who dared to criticize the chief executive or other officials could be jailed. People were in a fury about it. Vermont Congressman and editor Matthew Lyon was jailed for four months and charged $1,000 for accusing John Adams of having a thirst for ridiculous pomp and selfish avarice, among other things. In all, the Sedition Act led to 14 indictments, 11 trials, and 10 convictions. When Jefferson became president, he freed the journalists and allowed the law to lapse. An aggressive press, as irritating as it could be, was part of the great experiment.

It is impossible today to imagine a democratic country without freedom of the press. It is sometimes a great inconvenience to government, but that is a hallmark of a democratic system.

and Sam Adams of Massachusetts; George Clinton of New York; and Luther Martin of Maryland. They had made their careers in their colonies. They accused the Federalists of secretly wanting to create a monarchy. They did not believe that a republican form of government could work on a national scale. They did not think the rights of the individual were properly protected by the new Constitution. They felt that *they* were the true heirs of the spirit of the revolution. Neither group accepted the legitimacy of the other, which almost led to civil war.

The Anti-Federalists believed that no one would abandon farming to work in an urban area. There were vast acres of land, so they were convinced that a landless population would not develop the way it had in Europe. In their minds, there was more than enough to go around. This way of thinking proved to be wrong. Jefferson was an idealist; he believed that the people would not need government once they had been socialized. The Federalists thought the Anti-Federalists were a bunch of dreamers.

There were personal rivalries operating, too. In Virginia, Patrick Henry and James Madison were opposed to each other, and in New York, John Jay disliked Alexander Hamilton. Thomas Jefferson and John Adams had a friendship that warmed and cooled.

When the Anti-Federalists announced that they were going to demand another convention, the Federalists worked extra hard to push ratification through. It was now up to the American people to decide. It would not be a mass, public decision, but would be up to about 1,200

"GIVE ME LIBERTY, OR GIVE ME DEATH !"

Patrick Henry became an iconic figure during the American Revolutionary War in part because of his legendary speech in 1775. In order to raise support for the war, Henry spoke before the Virginia House of Burgesses, and concluded with the now famous line, "Give me liberty, or give me death!" The illustration above depicts Henry giving his speech and gaining the support of his fellow Virginians.

delegates elected to state conventions in hundreds of small contests across the 1,000-mile area of the United States. The future of the republic was out of the hands of the Framers and in the hands of local politicians from the American backlands. These men would need to read all the documents, follow the debates in the newspapers, and get themselves elected as delegates. It is a system that is still followed today.

THE *FEDERALIST PAPERS*

Thirty-two-year-old radical Federalist Alexander Hamilton had begun to offend people, especially Governor Clinton, who was strongly Anti-Federalist. Hamilton indulged in personal attacks and generated unfavorable publicity around the new Constitution. Madison and John Jay were in New York City when Hamilton began to publish a series of essays in support of his political views. He soon brought Madison and Jay in to help him. It was an extraordinary collaboration. Jay wrote on foreign policy, Madison about the shape and structure of the new government, and Hamilton about the inadequacies of the confederation. They wrote anonymously, collectively using the pseudonym "Publius." The essays appeared in the *New York Packet,* the *Independent Journal,* and other publications. They were quite popular. People began to understand that the Constitution could be amended, that it did provide for a government by the people, and that, practically, it was the best that could be had in an imperfect world.

THE OPPOSITE OPINION

Richard Lee Henry of Virginia wrote *Letters From the Federal Farmer to the Republican,* criticizing the Constitution for being undemocratic. The biggest complaint was that it offered no Bill of Rights. Other concerns were that it promoted a central government that was too strong and that the Constitution was an instrument for the rich and against the poor. The Anti-Federalists, with Governor Clinton of

Alexander Hamilton was a Federalist who believed in a strong central government and supported the newly drafted U.S. Constitution. In order to persuade Americans to ratify the Constitution, Hamilton collaborated with James Madison and John Jay to anonymously publish the *Federalist Papers*. A series of 85 articles published between 1787 and 1788, the *Federalist Papers* garnered support for the Constitution after explaining that it could be amended in the future.

New York, Thomas Jefferson, and other notables behind them, had enough followers to worry the Federalists.

RATIFICATION

Delaware became the first state to ratify the Constitution, in December 1787. Their vote was unanimous. Pennsylvania ratified next, and New Jersey was third. Georgia ratified in January 1788. Connecticut followed in that same month. Most of the eight newspapers in Boston praised the new Constitution. In February, Massachusetts ratified it but recommended that a bill of rights be added to protect the states from federal interference in individual liberties. New Hampshire came next, making it the ninth state to ratify. They also wanted a bill of rights. Those promoting the new Constitution realized, however, that without New York and Virginia ratifying, the new government could not succeed. Virginia was the link between the South and North, and New York was the hinge between the middle and northern states.

In Virginia, James Madison, Governor Edmund Randolph, and John Marshall led the struggle for ratification. It was a massive battle, with George Mason and Patrick Henry leading the Anti-Federalists. Jefferson and others were certain that had George Washington not stepped in to convince delegates to vote for ratification, it would not have happened. In June 1788, Virginia ratified by a narrow margin of 10 votes.

In New York, a showdown took place between Alexander Hamilton and Governor George Clinton. Finally, in

George Clinton *(above)* was governor of New York and an adamant Anti-Federalist. He was in favor of the states having the majority of power, and was opposed to the newly developed U.S. Constitution. He was against the ratification of the Constitution because it did not include a bill of rights and it created a strong centralized government.

July, New York ratified, with 30 yeas (approvals) and 27 nays. A bill of rights was recommended.

The Continental Congress passed a resolution on September 13, 1788, to put the new constitution into operation. Congress met for the first time under the new constitution on April 30, 1789. George Washington was elected the first president of the United States. North Carolina finally ratified in November 1789, and Rhode Island followed in May 1790.

Madison was elected to the first House of Representatives as a Federalist. He played a large part in forming the Departments of State, Treasury, and War. His biggest focus, however, was to promote a bill of rights, which would comprise the first 10 amendments to the Constitution. The division of powers between the federal and state governments was the toughest political challenge so far. All along, the Framers had referred to the creation of the American republic as an experiment. An uncertain future lay ahead. It was one thing to have prepared a document that worked on paper. The question remained, though, would it work in practice?

5

THOSE WHO
WERE LEFT OUT

Women, slaves, indentured servants, American Indians, and the poor were omitted from the Constitution. The issue of women and American Indians can be summed up in a sentence or two, as they were basically ignored during the writing of the Constitution. In a 1776 letter, Abigail Adams urged her husband, John Adams, to "remember the ladies," but he did not listen. Some of the members of the Constitutional Convention made it clear that giving the vote to dependent people—as women and other minorities were considered to be—was a potential source of instability.

After the Revolutionary War, black Americans, who made up one-fifth of the population, had almost no education and only a few of the basic necessities. Slaves worked for years with no pay and endured brutal treatment. Efforts had been made to keep them illiterate, and they had always been held in disdain by whites. The citizens of America generally believed that the slaves were not inferior biologically, but still looked down on them because they had no nurturing and no education.

TABOO ISSUE

Though the words *slave* or *slavery* are never mentioned in the Constitution, the topic was very much alive throughout the 1787 convention and afterward. One of the many problems of slavery was that there were 700,000 slaves in the United States, and that population continued to grow.

As early as the Revolutionary War, several schemes had come up whereby slaves would be freed and their owners compensated in return for enlistment in the conflict. Lafayette had suggested to Washington that he emancipate the slaves in Virginia and establish them in the western region as tenant farmers. Vermont in 1777 and New Hampshire in 1779 made slavery illegal in their state constitutions. Massachusetts declared slavery unconstitutional in 1783, Pennsylvania in 1780, and Rhode Island in 1784. Connecticut had an emancipation plan in 1784. It took New York and New Jersey longer, as they had the largest slave populations among the Northern states. Some of their slaves became indentured servants, but at least they knew they could be free one day.

In 1782, the Virginia legislature passed a law allowing slave owners to free their slaves if they wanted to. More than 12,000 freed slaves lived in the state by the

Abigail Adams *(above)* was a strong supporter of women's rights. She constantly urged her husband, John Adams, to think of women when contributing to the founding of the nation. Women, black Americans, American Indians, and the poor were considered "dependents" and were omitted from the Constitution.

end of the decade, which was encouraging. In his book *Notes on the State of Virginia,* Thomas Jefferson suggested that all slaves born after 1800 would eventually become free. In 1784 he proposed a bill in the federal Congress prohibiting slavery in all the western territories. It failed to pass by only one vote.

The 1787 convention included 10 provisions that dealt with slavery, even if the word was never used. The Southern states had large slave populations, which would give them an advantage when assigning seats in the House of Representatives. It was finally decided that each slave would count as only three-fifths of a person, and it was agreed that Congress could not end the slave trade before 1808.

Benjamin Franklin called for a statement of principle. He condemned both slavery and the slave trade. Several northern delegates convinced him to withdraw his proposal, saying that it put the Constitution at risk. The Southern states of Georgia and South Carolina were making threats to withdraw if they were told they had to let their slaves go. They wanted continued access to African slaves to stock their plantations, and they wanted free entry to western lands, with no federal restrictions on slavery in the territories. The Congress under the Articles of Confederation had passed the Northwest Ordinance in July 1787 and forbade slavery in the territory north of the Ohio River. The problem was that it could be read as a kind of approval of slavery in the southwestern region. Gouverneur Morris, who was a New Yorker but attended the convention as a delegate from Pennsylvania, proposed a national tax to compensate slave owners.

The delegates worried that, if the slavery question was indeed resolved, ratification would never happen. The North and the South made a deal. According to Joseph H. Ellis, author of *Founding Brothers: The Revolutionary Generation*,

This 1862 engraving depicts a typical slave auction. Although some of the Framers, such as Benjamin Franklin, condemned slavery, the slave trade continued well past their lifetimes.

The bargain entailed an exchange of votes whereby New England agreed to back an extension of the slave trade for twenty years in return for support from the Deep South for making the federal regulation of commerce a mere majority vote in the Congress rather than the usual two-thirds majority.

A MISSED OPPORTUNITY

In hindsight, the post-revolutionary period was the ideal time to abolish slavery. The leaders were aware of how it looked to be clinging to a slave society in light of the

Declaration of Independence. Vermont, Massachusetts, Pennsylvania, and North Carolina wanted it banned in the western areas in 1790. Religious leaders had started to condemn it. Although Georgia and South Carolina threatened to secede if the abolition of slavery became an issue, it is doubtful that they could have survived cut off from the rest of the country. In 1782, Georgia was described as devastated. Tens of thousands of slaves had died or joined the British during the war years. According to Gary B. Nash, while the state attempted to recover from the war, the Creek Indians began to attack and drove out the frontiersmen. Georgia and South Carolina desperately needed the union, so it seems strange that they had so much power concerning the issue of slavery.

England was in the process of abolishing the slave trade in 1791, and the French Revolutionary government emancipated half a million slaves in 1794. This led to an antislavery campaign in the United States in the 1790s. The American leaders thought the nation was too frail to handle such a change, however. Luther Martin of Maryland spoke up during the heated debates on ratifying the Constitution. He said,

> It ought to be considered that the continuance of the slave trade, and thus giving it a national sanction and encouragement ought to be considered as justly us to the displeasure and vengeance of Him, who is equal Lord of all, and who

views with equal eye, the poor African slave and his American master.

He withdrew from the Constitutional Convention and refused to sign the document because of it.

VIRGINIA

Virginia had 292,000 slaves and 12,000 freed slaves. Leaders from that state needed to lead the fight against their oppression. Although all the rhetoric coming from Virginia seemed in favor of abolishing the slave trade, many owners of slaves there were opposed to giving up control over their own slave populations.

It is surprising that the three men who had extraordinary influence, George Washington, Thomas Jefferson, and James Madison—all from the large state of Virginia, all of whom had expressed a hatred of the evil of slavery, all of whom were slave owners, all of whom had a huge influence over the people—would not become role models for others by setting free their own slaves. George Washington's neighbor, Robert Carter III, who was a member of the First Families of Virginia, decided to act. In 1791, he wrote a deed of gift that would free all of his 509 slaves who worked on 14 plantations. He allowed them to rename themselves and set them up with land of their own. Carter, who had joined a black church, had demonstrated that owning slaves was a choice, not a necessity.

Another important Virginian, Richard Randolph, son of Edmund Randolph, provided for the emancipation of all of his slaves in his will five years later. He also bequeathed to them 400 acres of his own land. Other prominent Virginians, including George Mason, Patrick Henry, and George Wythe, supported the abolition of slavery. George Wythe, who signed the Declaration of Independence, was a mentor to Jefferson. After his wife died in 1787, he freed her slaves.

Washington knew he could be an example to others. He had seen the bravery of the black soldiers who had fought for him in the Revolutionary War, and he admired them. In 1785, the issue of slavery went before Virginia's House of Delegates. A petition went out from Methodist leaders urging a gradual emancipation for slaves. Washington refused to sign, but agreed to write a letter to the House. The petition was rejected. Washington did not send the letter.

The Marquis de Lafayette of France had talked with Washington about freeing their country's slaves at the same time. Lafayette purchased an estate in New Guinea and began to settle French slaves there, and he invited Washington to join him. Washington wrote to him in 1786, still uncertain about what to do. Gary B. Nash, in his book, *The Forgotten Fifth*, wrote that Lafayette replied, "I would never have drawn my sword in the cause of America if I could have conceived thereby that I was founding a land of slavery." After Washington became president in 1790, he again talked about preparing some of his slaves for emancipation; in his second term, he spoke again about liberating his slaves, but he did nothing.

Jefferson also spoke against slavery in strong terms, calling it a "hideous blot" on civilized society. He was already an international symbol, and none of his actions would go unnoticed. Yet, when he became president in 1801, he was proslavery. When Jefferson organized the Louisiana Territory, he introduced a strong slave code. Some maintained that Jefferson wanted to be liked, and he knew if he brought the issue of emancipation of slaves to other slave owners, he would create a storm of protests. Even as late as 1817, when he was offered full compensation for 80 of the 230 slaves he owned, if he freed them, he refused to let them go. At Jefferson's death, he was so heavily in debt that all but five of his slaves were sold at auction.

Madison, too, claimed to hate slavery despite owning slaves. He knew that the new nation could not survive the stain of slavery, but he, too, could not force himself to act to abolish slavery. Psychologists who later studied the way these three American political giants turned their heads when the issue of slavery was brought up came to the conclusion that reputations and political power of all three rested on popular approval. It is thought that they limited their risk-taking as a result.

NORTHERNERS

Benjamin Franklin, although unwell, tried to fight against slavery by becoming president of the Pennsylvania Abolition Society and lending his name to a petition presented at the first Congress in 1790 to abolish the slave trade. A senator from Connecticut offered an amendment to the Constitution that would free male slaves by age 22, and female slaves by age 19, but it was voted down in the Senate.

John Adams tried to keep slavery off the reform agenda, even when his wife, Abigail, made it known that she was completely opposed to slavery. She urged her husband to oppose it more forcefully, but he was unwilling to take the risk. Northerners did not want to participate in solving the problems of slavery. Most Northern slaves had either

GEORGE WASHINGTON'S RUNAWAY SLAVES

Washington had 124 slaves at his estate in Virginia. Two, however, were special enough to be taken to Philadelphia when he became president. The first, Ona Judge, was the daughter of an enslaved seamstress at Mount Vernon. Her father was a white indentured servant from England. In 1784, when she was 10, this girl of mixed race began to serve Martha Washington. The second slave, Hercules, was the couple's prized cook and enjoyed a special status.

Washington wrote in a letter in 1791 that he did not believe his slaves would benefit from being freed. On the other hand, he worried that they might be tempted by freedom. In 1796, when Ona learned that Martha Washington was about to give her to her granddaughter, she fled the executive mansion. She had her things carried to a waiting ship and left while the Washingtons were at dinner. It was a potentially embarrassing situation. Washington sent agents to intercept her in Portsmouth, New Hampshire, her destination. Ona sent word that, if they guaranteed her freedom, she would return to them out of affection. They refused. They died or run away, and their children became indentured servants for 28 years before they could gain their freedom. Further, Northerners created a compromise that would keep them from having to pay much state duty on exports. Still, Adams and Franklin could have convinced their people of the need to abolish slavery as a means of keeping the union together.

At the first session of Congress, petitions delivered by Quakers and other groups opposing slavery were

were worried that their other slaves would hear of it and begin to make demands. People in Portsmouth heard about Ona, and finally the agent sent to bring her home reported that he feared a public outcry if he seized her. Two years later, the Washingtons sent their nephew, Burwell Bassett, after her, but to no avail. Ona had married and had a baby, and she finished out her life in New Hampshire as a free woman.

Only nine months after Ona left, Hercules, too, ran away. He had mingled with free blacks in Philadelphia. The promise of the American Revolution made him long for his own freedom. He slipped away from the president's house and made his way to New York, outwitting all of Washington's attempts to capture him. Washington did not have him tracked because he realized that the news that his slaves were running away would tarnish his reputation. He decided to add to his will that he wanted the slaves belonging to him freed after his death. Martha Washington had her own slaves, which were part of her dowry, and Washington had no authority over them.

addressed. The press brought the issues to the public. In the end, Madison said that Congress had "no authority to interfere in the emancipation of slaves, or in the treatment of them," according to Gary B. Nash, author of *The Forgotten Fifth*.

The realization that the revolutionary promise of an end to slavery was not going to happen was a bitter pill for many to swallow. Hindsight, as the saying goes, is always better than foresight. Thomas Jefferson became president in 1800. Sixty years later, some 600,000 Americans would die and many more would be injured in the American Civil War, which would be fought over the issue of slavery.

6

THE BIG
EXPERIMENT

Washington felt torn about being elected president, which was his normal response to any new role. He was continuing to live up to his reputation as a virtuous leader, but how would a new president act? He was not a king, even though many in the early years of his presidency thought that the office might slide into a monarchy. Others came right out and said they thought Washington should be president for life.

At age 57, he was inaugurated as the first president of the United States. The inauguration took place on April 30, 1789, in New York City. New York City was pro-Federalist, even though George Clinton, a strong Anti-Federalist, had been governor for 14 years. With a population of 33,000, New York had not yet caught up with Philadelphia, which was then the largest city in the country. Statistics showed that at that time, 29,700 New Yorkers were white, 2,400 were slaves, and the rest were free, nonwhite people. Washington was administered the oath of office by Chancellor Livingston, and after he had repeated the words, he lifted the Bible to his lips. John Adams was elected as the new vice president, a position he soon grew to dislike, as he did not like taking second place.

State representatives to the House of Representatives and the Senate were elected in the midst of a lot of conflict. The Federalists won in most states, including Virginia. An argument ensued immediately over how to address the president. Some wanted to call him "His Highness." They finally settled on the title "the President of the United States." He would be addressed as "Mr. President."

In 1789, the third arm of the new government was established. The Judiciary Act was passed, creating a Supreme Court to consist of a chief justice and five associates, 3 circuit courts, and 13 district courts. John Jay of New York became the first Chief Justice of the United States.

Washington gathered his friends around him as he went about creating the new government. Thomas Jefferson was made Secretary of State, Alexander Hamilton was Secretary of the Treasury, Henry Knox of Massachusetts was Secretary of War, and Edmund Randolph of Virginia was Attorney General. The men who had been instrumental in creating the new Constitution and having it ratified were now able to implement the new government. More than half the members of the 1787

John Jay was one of the Founding Fathers of the United States of America. A stalwart Federalist, John Jay coauthored the *Federalist Papers* with Alexander Hamilton and James Madison. George Washington appointed Jay as the first chief justice of the U.S. Supreme Court.

Constitutional Convention were appointed or elected legislators, judges, or administrators. All had a common goal of rapid economic development.

Washington worked hard to create a government that was respectable and dignified. He put a strong focus on ceremony because he knew the people wanted it. He kept 14 servants and 7 slaves in his house on Broadway. He had a carriage and 6 horses. He entertained with large dinners, serving champagne and expensive wines.

THE ECONOMY

It was Alexander Hamilton's time to shine. He was not born in what was to become the United States, but on the island of Nevis in the British West Indies in 1755. His father was Scottish, and his parents never married, which meant that the illegitimate Hamilton was never allowed to forget it. His father abandoned him, and his mother died when he was young. Hamilton was smart, and when he published an article in a local paper, friends who read it gave him the opportunity to acquire an education. He graduated from King's College (later renamed Columbia University).

Hamilton wanted the new government to assume the states' debts that were the result of the American Revolution. He presented many other bills concerning finances that began to alarm some of the legislators. They were reminded of their fear of a dominating national government that would create a paradise for speculators. It now felt like the people against the moneyed men. Hamilton was shocked when Madison, his partner in setting up the new government, was opposed to major parts of his report.

Hamilton negotiated with the Southerners about moving the capital of the new nation further south. Next, he wanted to create a powerful national bank. He believed in the power of money, calling it the "lifeblood of the economy." He would increase the amount of notes in circulation. In truth, he was trying to marry government and private bankers.

Hamilton's actions split Congress into warring factions again over the private control of a bank. Madison stepped up and announced that, after reviewing the Constitution, he found no power in it to incorporate a bank. It was also lacking powers to lay and collect taxes, borrow money, and pass laws in order to make it work. Washington turned to the Virginians, Jefferson and Randolph. They agreed with Madison that the Constitution did not give the federal government the power to establish a banking corporation, and no authority could be used to make it so. Madison was well on his way to switching from his Federalist stance to becoming Anti-Federalist. He would once again be on the side of Thomas Jefferson.

Hamilton wrote out a brilliant and broad construction of the Constitution. He insisted that the bank was vital to the collection of taxes and regulation of trade. He said that the federal government had the right to use all means to realize objectives that were not forbidden by the Constitution. Washington sided with him. It took Hamilton another two years, but he presented an economic plan to the United States. This was one of the first tests of the new Constitution.

BILL OF RIGHTS

During the first Congress, because of intense demand, Madison began to draft a bill of rights. It later became the first 10 amendments to the Constitution. The First Amendment guarantees freedom of speech, freedom of the press, and freedom of association and assembly. Citizens can also worship as they please, and they cannot be forced to support someone else's religion. Jefferson had written this into the Virginia Constitution much earlier. "Freedom of conscience" was one of the few things he wanted to be remembered for.

The Second Amendment is surrounded by controversy today. It announces the right of the people to keep and bear arms. Some think this affirms a broad individual right to gun ownership, whereas others think it protects only a narrow right to possess firearms as members of a militia. The Third Amendment rarely comes up today. It says that no soldier in times of peace can be kept in any house without the consent of the owner. The Fourth Amendment makes it clear that the police and other government officials cannot search people's home or offices, or seize their property, without reasonable grounds to believe that a crime has been committed. In most cases, officials have to get a written warrant from a judge in order to conduct a search. The Fifth Amendment protects people against arbitrary government actions. Amendments Six through Eight protect those accused of crimes. The Ninth Amendment states that courts cannot assume that, if the Constitution does not list a right, there is no such right to protect individuals from the government. The Tenth Amendment states that,

In December 1791, the Bill of Rights was added to the U.S. Constitution. The Bill of Rights consists of the first 10 amendments to the Constitution, and covers freedom of speech, religion, and the press, as well as the controversial right to bear arms.

if a particular power was not assigned to the federal government by the Constitution, the states may exercise the power, unless the Constitution forbids it.

In December 1791, the 10 ratified amendments that formed the Bill of Rights were added to the end of the Constitution. Today, the Bill of Rights is one of the most recognizable parts of the Constitution. To create it, however, Washington and his colleagues had to start with more than 200 amendments submitted by state ratifying conventions.

By 1792, it was obvious that George Washington would remain in power for another four years. John Adams was voted in again as vice president. The government of the United States of America seemed to be working. For the moment, the Framers could breathe a sigh of relief.

THE FINAL CHAPTER OF THE FOUNDERS' LIVES

Washington left office in 1797, a decade after the Constitutional Convention. The Federalists and the Democratic-Republicans made peace with each other, at least temporarily. Washington gave a masterful farewell speech when he decided to leave, which today is considered an important political document. Then, he went home to Mount Vernon. He accepted command of the army when it looked as if America might be going to war with France in 1798, but that did not happen, so he again returned to Mount Vernon. He became ill and died there on December 14, 1799. He was 66 years old.

John Adams was elected the second president of the United States in 1796. He didn't appoint a new cabinet, and cabinet members turned to Washington rather than to him for guidance. He defied them and the Federalist Party when he made peace with France. Adams was not elected to a second term. He never lost his pessimistic view of societies. He never understood letting sovereignty rest with the people. Elected officials were agents of the people, which was the opposite of what Adams believed the system should be. Critics and fellow politicians, who saw Adams trying to sow seeds of discontent, criticized his book *Defence of the Constitutions of the United States.* They thought him obsessed with aristocracy. He became quite separated from his countrymen. At age 79, Adams was still arguing his points. He was accused of being old fashioned and out of touch with what America was really about. One critic said that his work was more a caricature of the Constitution than a defense. Adams died feeling misunderstood.

Thomas Jefferson was unhappy in the Washington administration and finally resigned. In 1796, he became vice president under John Adams. He hated the way Adams was running the government and decided to make it his goal to become president in 1800. He succeeded, and although the Federalists remained opposed to him, he was popular with the people. His biggest success during those years was the Louisiana Purchase, in 1803. He also managed to reduce taxes and cut the military budget. He won the election of 1804 easily. The Lewis and Clark Expedition returned triumphant. He tried to use economic pressure against England and France, who were violating American sovereignty. He created the Embargo Act, which prohibited all exports and most imports. The Federalists, who had all but disappeared, roared back into politics. During the last 17 years of Jefferson's life, he put all of his

(Continued on page 78)

SEAT OF POWER

★ ★ ★ ★ ★

At first, the federal government was located in Philadelphia; then, its location shifted to New York. The time came, however, when a decision had to be made about its permanent home. Southerners thought Hamilton's financial proposals (a national bank, etc.) favored eastern interests over theirs, and it looked like he would not get them passed. As much as he wanted the nation's capital to remain in New York, he wanted even more for his financial report to be approved. So, he offered a deal: If the Southerners approved his proposals, he would offer support for a southern location for the capital. He was successful. In August 1790, his Report on Public Credit was approved by a narrow margin, and it was agreed that the capital would move to Philadelphia for 10 years, then relocate to a spot on the banks of the Potomac River in Virginia.

George Washington chose the site for the capital city, which was named after him. Jefferson talked his colleagues into naming it after their first president. Jefferson was also responsible for calling the district Columbia and the legislative seat of government the Capitol. Although Jefferson jumped right in with designs, one of Washington's French war friends, Major Pierre Charles L'Enfant, came and suggested 160-foot-wide boulevards that would carry the names of the states. To finance the venture, instead of charging everything to the government, Washington, Jefferson, and Madison held an auction in which 10,000 lots were put up for sale. Only 35 sold. This happened three times in all and became an embarrassment. Some people stepped in and made huge donations, but when the government was moved there in 1800, there were only 372 structures in the new district.

A competition was held to build the new presidential residence. Nine proposals were made, and Irish-born James Hoban won.

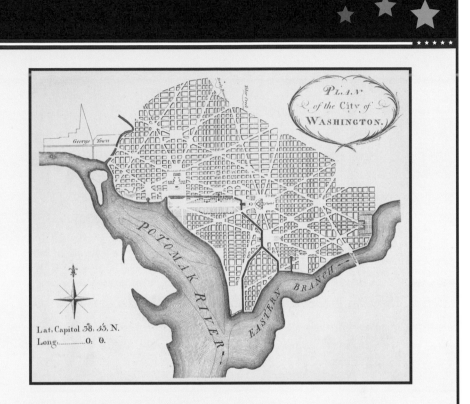

The image above shows Pierre-Charles L'Enfant's plan of the city of Washington. Chief architect L'Enfant designed a grid pattern for the streets with avenues connecting the city's important landmarks.

Construction started in 1792. President Washington oversaw the construction of the White House but never lived in it. President John Adams and his wife Abigail were the first to occupy it.

Thomas Jefferson held the White House's first inaugural open house in 1805. He also opened it to public tours. The tradition of

(continues)

(continued)

the open house held until after Lincoln's presidency, when in-augural crowds became too large. The British set fire to the building in 1814, during the War of 1812, but the structure survived. Even 20 years later, the population of the city was fewer than 10,000. The entire federal headquarters numbered only 291 people in 1802, when Jefferson was president.

Today, the White House stands regally as a symbol of the presidency, the United States government, and the Ameri-can people. On January 21, 1993, President Clinton held an open house. Two thousand citizens, selected by lottery, were greeted in the Diplomatic Reception area by the president; his wife, Hillary Rodham Clinton; and Vice President Al Gore and his wife, Tipper.

(Continued from page 75)

energy into creating the University of Virginia. Among his many accomplishments, he wanted to be remembered for only three: freedom from Britain, freedom of conscience, and freedom maintained through education. He died on July 4, 1826, at Monticello.

Madison was elected president in 1808. He was not as successful a leader as Jefferson. He asked for and received a declaration of war on Britain in June of 1812, starting the War of 1812. He became disheartened over the prog-ress of that war. America was on the verge of bankruptcy, too. Madison fell ill a year later, but after the British were defeated, his health improved. He retired to his beloved Montpellier and worked with Jefferson to found the University of Virginia. He was bedridden in his final years, and died on June 28, 1836.

Benjamin Franklin died in 1790. He received only one public eulogy, and that was by an enemy, William Smith, who was head of the American Philosophical Society. He apologized for Franklin's humble beginnings. The French, however, did not hold back. They delivered eulogies and proclaimed three days of mourning. When the House of Representatives asked the Senate to join them in endorsing a resolution honoring Franklin, the Senate refused. Only after his death, and the publication of his autobiography, did his image change. He became a role model for the self-made man, someone who had shaped his own destiny.

It was Alexander Hamilton who wrote Washington's farewell address in 1796. After Washington died, the leadership of the Federalist Party was divided between Adams and Hamilton. Hamilton, however, was not as popular as Adams. He spoke his mind, and was self-confident and uncompromising by nature. After John Adams was elected president, Hamilton stepped in to control policy. In 1800 he wrote an attack against the president that was intended for private circulation. It landed in the hands of Aaron Burr, Hamilton's rival, however. The two men had competed with each other for a long time. Hamilton thwarted Burr's every move to climb the political ladder.

The acquisition known as the Louisiana Purchase cost the
United States $15 million—approximately 4 cents an acre—in
1803. With this transaction, the United States doubled in size
and began its westward expansion. The map above shows
the land included in the purchase.

Burr forced a quarrel and challenged Hamilton to a duel.
It was fought at Weehawken on the New Jersey shore on
July 11, 1804. Hamilton was shot, and died the following
day. Ironically, Hamilton's son Philip had died in a duel
in 1801.

Each of these men lived long enough to see his work
on the Constitution in action. Although they all suffered
disappointments, they knew that, by the end of their lives,
they had been instrumental in creating a masterpiece.

7

THE CONSTITUTION TODAY

The U.S. Constitution has been in effect for more than 200 years. The Framers believed that the best government would exist by the consent of the governed. The Constitution stated that sovereignty resided with the people, not with the federal government or the individual states. At the time the Constitution was written, there was no such thing as the "American people"—only scattered groups of people that needed to be brought into a larger whole. There was no common history as a nation and no common experience except for, of course, the Revolutionary War. The desire for independence existed, however, in the hearts of immigrants who had made their way to America.

When the Framers spoke of liberty, they meant civil liberty, not natural liberty. Natural liberty meant that the individual could do whatever he wanted. Civil liberty meant freedom of action as long as it was not harmful to others. When the Framers talked about political liberty, they were talking about the freedom to vote and to hold public office.

A CONTRAST IN INTERPRETATION OF THE CONSTITUTION

Chief Justice John Marshall sat on the Supreme Court from 1801, when Jefferson was elected president, until his death in 1835. Jefferson could not stand him. It was Marshall who decided that it was up to the courts, not other branches of government, to say what the Constitution means. The Supreme Court became the interpreter of the Constitution. It was that Supreme Court that ruled, for example, that Congress could create a bank, using a clause that said Congress could take whatever actions it needed to achieve its legitimate goals. In this case, it was about regulating the economy. On the other hand, the Supreme Court could not force other branches of government to obey its decisions. In 1957, when some Southern states were still ignoring the 1954 desegregation ruling, President Dwight Eisenhower sent federal troops in to enforce it. That is a rare occurrence.

The president appoints the justices of the Supreme Court. Today, if the president is a Republican, then generally he or she will appoint more conservative justices, and if the president is a Democrat, the justices will be more liberal. As Senator Patrick Leahy of Vermont said in 2005, "The appointment of justices of the Supreme Court will affect you, your children, your grandchildren, and your great-grandchildren." Their decisions have that much power.

AN ONGOING DEBATE

Jethro K. Lieberman, writing for Encarta Online Encyclopedia, explained, "The success of the Constitution lies in its flexibility. But it is flexible because it speaks in broad and sometimes murky phrases." It has to be subject to judicial interpretation. The question is, how to interpret it? Debates and arguments have been ongoing since the Constitution was ratified. Some believe the words of the Constitution should be read narrowly, whereas others believe that the words themselves should provide no guide to the outcome of a case. This is called a broad reading. A twentieth-century example is the case of *Roe v. Wade*, which protected a woman's right to have an abortion. Strict constructionists, who read narrowly, find no right to abortion. In the case of capital punishment, another hot issue, a broad reading would make capital punishment unconstitutional, but it was given a strict reading, which makes it allowable. Generally, strict constructionists are politically conservative, although that is not always true.

Dahlia Lithwick, an author for the Web site *Slate* wrote, "A country's constitution is only as useful as the tools that will be used to interpret it later." Many people in the United States today believe that there is only one way to view the Constitution, and that is in the way the

Framers first intended. This is referred to as originalism, and "strict construction."

Much of the popular belief is a reaction to the notion that the Constitution could be given different interpretations, according to the spirit of the times. In 1985, Attorney General Edwin Meese III, under President Ronald Reagan, began to challenge the view of constitutional jurisprudence. He implored judges to embrace instead a "jurisprudence of original intention."

Those who support the original intent of the Framers argue that the Constitution means exactly what the Framers intended it to mean in 1787. For example, if they said that the death penalty could be used, then it cannot be unconstitutional. The problem with strict construction is that it is impossible to know exactly what the Framers intended because they knew nothing of the modern world. In addition, which Framers should one look to? They themselves disagreed on many issues. They wrote the Constitution in such a way that it has many different meanings.

Finally, what about the leaders who ratified the Constitution? The truth is that no one can say what the single intent was of hundreds of people who happened to come together at the same time in state ratifying conventions. They left no records. There is no evidence that the Framers wanted citizens to refer to original intent. Furthermore, the Constitution does not say how it should be interpreted. What is clear is that the meaning of the Constitution changes with the times.

Historian Vic Henningsen, speaking on Vermont Public Radio in January of 2006, said, "There is a popular and puzzling argument that we can interpret the Constitution correctly only by understanding the intention of the framers when they created it. This is popular with many conservatives, who see it as a necessary antidote to overly broad rulings by overly liberal judges."

It must be remembered, he pointed out, that the Framers themselves disagreed about their intentions. The Constitution, after all, had only outlined the new system of government. In fact, Thomas Jefferson defined the concept of strict construction in a debate with Alexander Hamilton. Jefferson said that if the Constitution did not specifically grant a power, Congress did not have it. Hamilton disagreed, saying that Article I gave Congress broad implied powers. The argument has raged ever since. It has been noted that Jefferson was a strict constructionist while he was out of power and more of a broad constructionist when in power.

Henningsen pointed out that, as an elderly man, Jefferson changed again. Jefferson wrote:

> Some men look at Constitutions with sanctimonious reverence, and deem them like the arc of the covenant, too sacred to be touched. They ascribe to the men of the preceding age a wisdom more than human, and suppose what they did to be beyond amendment. I knew that age well; I belonged to it . . . it was very like the present, but without the experience of the present; and forty years of experience in government is worth a century of book-reading; and this they would say for themselves, were they to rise from the dead.

Jefferson continued,

> Laws and institutions must go hand in hand
> with the progress of the human mind. As that
> becomes more developed, more enlightened, as
> new discoveries are made, new truths disclosed,
> and manners and opinions change with the
> change in circumstances, institutions must ad-
> vance also, and keep pace with the times.

Only 27 amendments have made it all the way to ratification since the Constitution was first written. The first
10, called the Bill of Rights, were ratified in 1804. Some issues, such as the balance of authority between state governments and the federal government, are as unsettled
as they were when the Constitution was first adopted.
The debate over abortion continues. Privacy rights on the
Internet is only one of many modern issues that require
the courts to adapt and interpret the Constitution. Saul K.
Padover covered 60 Supreme Court decisions in his book
The Living U.S. Constitution, and he said they prove that
there is no "last word" when it comes to the Constitution.

CHANGES FOR AMERICA'S SECOND-CLASS CITIZENS

The Founders were right to worry about slavery rearing its
ugly head in the future. The clash between Southern de-
termination and Northern defensiveness exploded at Fort
Sumter on April 12, 1861. The Southerners had a string
of brilliant victories behind them by 1862, and President

Abraham Lincoln, the sixteenth president of the United States, was responsible for abolishing slavery. Lincoln worked to preserve the Union by defeating the Confederacy in the American Civil War. He is regarded as one of the greatest presidents in U.S. history.

Abraham Lincoln was torn. "Was it possible to lose the nation and yet preserve the Constitution?" he asked. Lincoln felt driven by circumstances to use arbitrary power. He did not call Congress into an emergency session until weeks after the battle at Fort Sumter. Instead, he called for more volunteers, spent money, declared a blockage, and suspended habeas corpus. When Congress met in July, however, Lincoln received all the support he needed to enter wholeheartedly into the war.

As James MacGregor Burns recorded in his book *The Vineyard of Liberty*, Lincoln declared when he was criticized for putting down the rebellion instead of ridding the South of slavery, "My paramount object in this struggle is to save the Union and is not either to save or destroy slavery. If I could save the Union without freeing any slave I would do it, and if I could save it by freeing all the slaves I would do it."

It was only as the war lagged that the subject of abolition took a front seat. Finally, Lincoln decided to issue a general emancipation, but not until he had won the war. After the Battle of Antietam, the president issued his decree. In 100 days—on January 1, 1863, all slaves in any states or area still in rebellion would be declared free. The Fifteenth Amendment of the U.S. Constitution was ratified on February 3, 1870. It said that neither state governments nor the federal government can stop people from voting because of their race or because they were once slaves. It was enforced for a brief time in the 1870s, and after that not until the 1960s, when the civil rights movement brought black Americans to the polls.

In 1848, two women, Lucretia Mott and Elizabeth Cady Stanton, led the "Women's Rights Convention" held in Seneca Falls, New York. They launched the women's suffrage movement (which promoted voting rights for women). After many marches, rallies, pickets, and hunger strikes, the Nineteenth Amendment passed in 1920, giving women the right to vote. It had taken more than 70 years since the convention in 1848. Patricia Ireland, president of the National Organization for Women, was quoted as saying, "During the first 200 years of our country's history, the Supreme Court justices never saw a discriminatory law against women they didn't like." Supreme Court decisions centering on women's rights have not been consistent. In 1961, the justices upheld Florida's exclusion of women from jury duty because women were the center of home and family life.

In 1971, attorney Ruth Bader Ginsburg made a breakthrough for women with regard to gender discrimination. Idaho had a law that automatically gave preference to a man over an equally qualified woman when appointing the person responsible for disposing of the property of someone who has died. Ginsburg had the law thrown out. She became the second woman appointed to the Supreme Court and today is the only woman serving.

AN EXTRAORDINARY DOCUMENT

Historians, whether they glorify or criticize the U.S. Constitution, all agree that it is unique in its success. Historian Walter A. McDougal, in his book titled *Freedom Just*

(Continued on page 92)

TESTING THE LIMITS

★ ★ ★ ★ ★

Many presidents, including Ronald Reagan, George H.W. Bush, Bill Clinton, and George W. Bush, have all tested the limits of the Constitution. Charlie Savage, writing for *The Boston Globe*, said that "President [George W.] Bush has quietly claimed the authority to disobey more than 750 laws enacted since he took office, asserting that he has the power to set aside any statute passed by Congress when it conflicts with his interpretation of the Constitution." According to certain legal scholars, Bush worked to expand his power and thus upset the balance of power among the branches of government. More than any previous president, Bush has declared his right to ignore many laws. He claims they interrupt the power he believes the Constitution assigns to him alone.

Some say that George W. Bush positioned himself as the ultimate interpreter of the Constitution. He rarely uses his presidential power to veto bills he disagrees with. Instead, he has signed most of them, but when the official signing is over, he quietly files "signing statements," asserting that the Constitution gives him the right to ignore large sections of the bills. The public has little idea this is happening. For example, Congress has passed bills forbidding U.S. troops from fighting in Colombia. After Bush signed the bill, in his "signing statement," he claimed that he did not have to obey the restrictions because he is commander in chief of the military.

Bush's abuse of power came up in August 2006 when a federal judge ruled that the U.S. government's domestic eavesdropping program was unconstitutional and ordered it ended immediately. The administration had secretly given the National Security Administration permission to conduct wiretaps without a court order.

New York University law professor David Golove said that Bush has cast a cloud over the whole idea that there is a rule of law. Which laws, for example, does he think he can ignore and which ones does he think are valid? Golove worries that Bush threatens to "overturn the existing structures of constitutional law." The Constitution, Golove says, could disappear if the president ignores the Court and has a Congress unwilling to challenge him.

President Ronald Reagan started the practice of "signing statements" when his attorney general, Edwin Meese, decided that such statements could be used to increase the president's power. George H.W. Bush challenged 232 statutes in four years, and Bill Clinton objected to 140 laws over eight years. They used the presidential veto if they had a serious problem with a bill, however, which gave Congress a chance to override their decisions.

After the September 11, 2001, attacks on America, President Bush used national security issues as a reason to keep his actions hidden. Jack Beermann, professor of law at Boston University, said, "The president is daring Congress to act against his positions, and they're not taking action because they don't want to appear to be too critical of the president, given that their own fortunes are tied to his because they are all Republicans." A deputy attorney general in the Reagan administration said, "This is an attempt by the president to have the final word on his own constitutional powers, which eliminates the checks and balances that keep the country a democracy. . . . [T]his is moving us toward an unlimited executive power."

(Continued from page 89)

Around the Corner: A New American History, wrote, "The creation of the United States of America is the central event of the past four hundred years."

The United States is now the oldest enduring republic in world history. Although the republican model—representative government using the principle of popular sovereignty—is the norm today, no country that had tried it previously had succeeded. Even in the United States, there were times when the Founders felt like throwing up their hands. Joseph J. Ellis, author of *Founding Brothers: The Revolutionary Generation,* wrote that John Adams, who devoted most of his life to the Constitution and the new republic complained when the idea of a new constitution was put forth: "Who can legislate for 20 or 30 states, each of which is greater than Greece or Rome at those times?" We might ask, who indeed?

Jefferson and Adams corresponded throughout their lives. As elderly men who were close to death, they spoke about the American Revolution and its aftermath. Jefferson saw it as an explosion "that dislodged America from England, from Europe, from the past itself, the opening shot in a global struggle for liberation from all forms of oppression that was destined to sweep around the world." It was a big bang theory, and would spread throughout the world naturally.

Adams, when asked for a toast at a local celebration in Quincy, said, "Independence Forever." When asked about his views about the American Revolution, his thoughts were the opposite of Jefferson's. To him, the American Revolution was still an experiment. Public opinion was unpredictable, yet the authority of the republican government rested on the opinions of the people.

The two political giants died on the same day—July 4, 1826. On July 3, Jefferson, very ill, whispered, "Is it the Fourth?" He lingered until the next day. Adams collapsed in his favorite reading chair on that same day, becoming unconscious at the same time that Jefferson took his last breath. His last words were, "Thomas Jefferson survives," or according to someone else's account, "Thomas Jefferson still lives." We could say that both remain alive in the words of the U.S. Constitution.

GLOSSARY

amendment A formal change to the United States Constitution.

bicameral Composed of two houses, as in a legislature.

Bill of Rights The first 10 amendments, which were adopted in 1791. The basic rights that all Americans have are contained within them.

checks and balances The three branches of the government—the executive, legislative, and judicial—have the power to check each other in order to maintain a "balance" of power.

constitution A document that contains the rules a country or a state must follow. The Constitution of the United States is the highest law. It was handwritten on only four pages.

democracy The name comes from the Greek word, *demokratia*, a combination of *demos*, meaning "people," and *kratos*, meaning "rule." Democracy is a philosophy in which the people ideally have a lot of control over political leaders. Democracy is based on the belief that all should have the same basic rights and freedoms.

executive branch The branch of government made up of the president, the vice president, the president's staff, executive agencies, and Cabinet departments, such as the State Department, the Department of Defense, and others.

federalism   Division of power between the national government and the state governments.

Founding Fathers (also, Founders)   Refers to those who played a significant role in the creation of the United States of America and the Constitution.

Framers   Those who helped to write the Constitution, including George Washington, Benjamin Franklin, James Madison, and others.

The Great Compromise   Roger Sherman, a Connecticut delegate to the Constitutional Convention, wrote the proposal that called for proportional representation in the House of Representatives, and one representative per state in the Senate (later changed to two).

House of Representatives   Referred to as the "lower house." States are represented in the House based on population. Today, 435 representatives make up this body.

judicial branch   Responsible for interpreting the law. It includes all the federal courts, all the way up to the Supreme Court. State courts are under the national courts.

legislative branch   Called Congress. Members of Congress make laws, impose taxes, and borrow money. The legislative branch is split into the House of Representatives and the Senate.

republic   A type of government whereby the people control the government through elected political officials who make laws for the country. Also referred to as indirect democracy and representative government.

rule of law A doctrine that states that all people are equal before the law, and the government is subject to this law. It is one of the great legacies of the constitutional system.

Senate The "upper house" that contains two representatives from each state. Today, 100 members make up the Senate.

separation of powers The idea that each of the three branches of government have their own power.

The United States of America The formal term was first used in the Declaration of Independence.

BIBLIOGRAPHY

Books

Burns, James MacGregor. *The Vineyard of Liberty*. New York: Alfred A. Knopf, 1982.

Ellis, Joseph J. *Founding Brothers: The Revolutionary Generation*. New York: Vintage Books, 2000.

Kammen, Michael, ed. *The Origins of the American Revolution: A Documentary History*. New York: Penguin Books, 1986.

McCullough, David. *John Adams*. New York: Simon & Schuster, 2001.

McDougall, Walter A. *Freedom Just Around the Corner: A New American History*. New York: Harper Perennial, 2004.

Meese III, Edwin. *The Heritage Guide to the Constitution*. Washington, D.C.: Regnery, 2005.

Nash, Gary B. *The Forgotten Fifth: African Americans in the Age of Revolution*. Cambridge, Mass., and London: Harvard University Press, 2006.

Oates, Stephen B. *Portrait of America*, 4th ed., vol. I. New York: Houghton-Mifflin, 1987.

Padover, Saul K. *The Living U.S. Constitution*. New York: Penguin, 1995.

Rakove, Jack N. *Original Meanings: Politics and Ideas in the Making of the Constitution*. New York: Vintage Books, 1996.

Wood, Gordon S. *Revolutionary Characters: What Made the Founders Different*. New York: Penguin, 2006.

Zinn, Howard. *A People's History of the United States*. New York: Harper Perennial, 1980.

Web Sites

America's Story From America's Library: Library of Congress.
http://www.americaslibrary.gov

The American Presidency
http://ap.grolier.com

Archiving Early America
http://www.earlyamerica.com

The James Madison Center
http://www.jmu.edu/madison/center

Our Documents Home
http://www.ourdocuments.gov

The Supreme Court Historical Society
http://www.supremecourthistory.org

The U.S. Constitution Online
http://www.usconstitution.net

U.S. National Archives and Records Administration
http://www.archives.gov

Virginia Historical Society
http://www.vahistorical.org

FURTHER READING

Books

Chall, Marsha Wilson. *Happy Birthday, America!* New York: HarperCollins, 2000.

Fink, Sam. *The Declaration of Independence.* New York: Scholastic, 2000.

Fritz, Jean. *Shh! We're Writing the Constitution.* New York: Putnam, 1987.

Web Sites

About: U.S. Gov Info/Resources
http://usgovinfo.about.com/blcnostday.htm

Education World
http:www.educationworld.com

**"Teaching With Documents: Observing Constitution Day,"
The National Archives**
http:www.archives.gov/education/lessons/constitution-day/

The U.S. Constitution Online
http://www.usconstitution.net

PICTURE CREDITS

11:   Library of Congress, cph-3b27098

13:   Art Resource, NY

15:   National Archives, Constitution, Pg 1 of 4 AC

20:   SMGraphics

22:   National Archives, Declaration, Pg 1 of 1 AC

29:   © Joseph Sohm/Fisions of America/Corbis

34:   Art Resource, NY

36:   Library of Congress, cph-3b49887

41:   Library of Congress, cph-3a53276u

43:   Library of Congress, cph-3b01947

49:   Library of Congress, cph-3b50326

51:   Library of Congress, cph-3b42378

53:   Library of Congress, cph-3c10647

57:   Library of Congress, cph-3b04614

59:   Art Resource, NY

69:   Library of Congress, cph-3b42488

73:   National Archives, Bill of rights, pg 1 of 1 AC

77:   Art Resource, NY

80:   SMGraphics

87:   Library of Congress, cph-3a11367

cover   The Granger Collection, New York

INDEX

ABOUT THE AUTHOR

JANET HUBBARD-BROWN has written about subjects as diverse as the Shawnee, NASCAR race drivers, and Geoffrey Chaucer for Chelsea House. She lives in Fayston, Vermont, where she works as a writer, an editor, and a teacher.